LEVITICUS
A Study of the Holiness of God

GILL
MINISTRIES

14122 Susancrest, San Antonio, TX 78232
E-mail: gministries@gmail.com
© Copyright 2005
ISBN # 1-931178-36-4
Vision Publishing
www.visionpublishingservices.com

Acknowledgements

This work is the culmination of several years of teaching Bible students at the post-secondary level. For much of that time I have revisited the Pentateuch each year. Although Genesis is my favorite book of the five that constitute this group, I have a deep affection for the book of Leviticus and have found it to hold a wealth of applications for New Testament believers.

I found that students benefited greatly from copies of my teaching notes while participating in the course. Therefore, I have sought to expand those notes so that they might be readable for any Bible student. Since they were developed and refined over such a long period of time it required much editing to make them a cohesive whole that could be publicly disseminated.

I am deeply grateful to many people for their help in producing this volume. The many students I have had the privilege of teaching gave me much helpful feedback. My colleagues have patiently listened and given beneficial comments, especially Dr. Al Reimer. I am most grateful to Scott Stripling who interrupted his very busy schedule to proof and edit the materials. Any mistakes belong to me and there would have been an abundance of them had it not been for Scott's work.

My family has been a constant support. Rebecca and Christy are fine adults who have been a source of consistent delight to their mother and me. They are true sounding boards helping me measure the waters I have sought to navigate. Sherry, my faithful companion and helper for many years never ceases to support my ministry through prayer and steadfastness. My parents, Fred and Marjorie, have always stood in the gap for me. They are great Christian models, but the true secret of their support has been their unceasing prayer for me. Finally, the support and help from my friend, my Barnabas, David Cook, has allowed me to unrelentingly pursue my studies.

Of course, without the Holy Spirit speaking to my spirit nothing is knowable or understandable. Without Him I am useless and handicapped indeed.

I pray that this brief work will bless you and enable you to enjoy a book that for many is very difficult and boring. It is neither of those two things and it is my goal to help you enjoy and appreciate this book about holiness.

Table of Contents

Figures

LEVITICUS
A Study of the Holy
By Van G. Gill

This is one of those books that most non-Jewish persons find difficult to read. It is not a narrative in the sense of story telling. It is an explanation. It explains God's mind concerning the covenant He made with Israel at Mt. Sinai. We have few things we can use for comparison and therefore it is difficult for us envision the contents of the book. Most of us do not live where sacrifices are made and it is difficult for us to put ourselves in the text, seeing and feeling it.

A second and more deadly hindrance to our comprehension of this book is the notion that the Old Testament is of very little value to people who are under the New Covenant. This could not be further from the truth. The only Scriptures available to our Lord and to the early church were those from to which we refer as the "Old Testament." Never forget that the roots of the Christian faith are Jewish. We are grafted into the cultivated, domestic tree. We were of the wild olive tree, and have been grafted onto the stump and roots of the cultivated one (Jewish and Old Testament). It is as we come to understand God's mind as established in these Old Testament pictures that we find hidden manna about New Testament truth.

It is a grievous error to impose a western, gentile way of viewing and explaining these wonderful Old Testament truths. If one takes the time to understand these things, one will find the New Testament more brilliant and lively.

The topics given in Leviticus are not some kind of parenthesis or stopgap measure. They are within God's plan and purpose. Blessed is the one who reads and understands.

THINKING ABOUT THE OLD TESTAMENT
The Old Testament Message and the Man who Receives It

For we know that the Law is spiritual; but I am of flesh, sold into bondage to sin. Rom 7:14 NAS

The "Law" is a way of saying "the Old Testament Message." Here it is described as being "spiritual." That is to say, it is not fleshly, carnal or natural. But, I am of flesh; that is, the person receiving the message was not spiritual. The Spirit of God did not indwell him. This means that God had a major problem. The problem occurred when He tried to communicate with the Old Testament person (OT man). In fact, under those conditions He could not communicate with him.

Now we have received, not the spirit of the world, but the Spirit who is from God, that we might know the things freely given to us by God, which things we also speak, not in words taught by human wisdom, but in those taught by the Spirit, combining spiritual thoughts with spiritual words. But a natural man does not accept the things of the Spirit of God; for they are foolishness to him, and he cannot understand them, because they are spiritually appraised. 1 Corinthians 2:12-14 NAS

A spiritual message is "taught by the Spirit" and the "natural" or carnal man does not accept or receive the things of the Spirit of God. If the message is spiritual and the natural man (OT man) cannot receive it, how can God communicate with that person?

Ideally, God would place His Spirit in a person so that he could understand and receive the message God wanted to give. However, this will not be an option until Christ will have come, will have returned to the Father and will have sent the Comforter to enter the person. This did occur on the Day of Pentecost in Acts 2. God still had a problem in the Old Testament. It was a problem of communication with man. He could not do in the man in the Old Testament what was needed to equip him to receive a spiritual message. So, God's only option was to do something to the message that would place it on a level where the Old Testament man could understand and receive it.

Upon which level would the message need to be for the goal of communication to be accomplished? It must be the same level upon which the person functions. The person is on a physical level (not spiritual) and therefore can only comprehend and communicate at that level. This means that this spiritual message must be "clothed" in the language and pictures of physical things: days, new moons, Sabbath days, foods, decaying things, etc. The problem is that the language about the physical obscures the spiritual intent of the message.

The message about defilement never was intended to be about foods and dead matter. Those things are the physical things. Jesus said that it is not what goes into the stomach that defiles, but what comes out of the heart and mouth that defiles.[1] When

---

[1] Mark 7:14-23

did the heart and mouth become the issue? When did foods and dead matter stop being what God intended? God's true intent was the same from the beginning. He could not speak to the OT man about it because that man could not receive such a message.

Confusion about the Old Testament message occurs when a student tries to make the message in its language about the physical to be its spiritual intent. The physical is a picture of the spiritual but is not the spiritual (the substance as Paul explains in the book of Colossians 2:16-17).

Therefore let no one act as your judge in regard to food or drink or in respect to a festival or a new moon or a Sabbath day-- things which are a mere shadow of what is to come; but the substance belongs to Christ. NAS

So, we will try to keep this principle of interpretation in mind. The Old Testament message comes to us in the clothing of the physical and about physical things. These things are not the substance that God wants us to see ultimately. It is the substance and not the shadow that is important to our studies.

The Mystery

A second principle of interpretation for Old Testament study is the principle of "the mystery." The mystery refers to something that was secret. The Old Testament scriptures are about something that was secret even to those used to transmit the message to readers and hearers, so that both the writers and the readers did not have a clue about what was really being said.

Consider the following passages:.
Now to Him who is able to establish you according to my gospel and the preaching of Jesus Christ, according to the revelation of the mystery which has been kept secret for long ages past, but now is manifested, and by the Scriptures of the prophets, according to the commandment of the eternal God, has been made known to all the nations, leading to obedience of faith; Romans 16:25-27 NAS

and to bring to light what is the administration of the mystery which for ages has been hidden in God, who created all things; Ephesians 3:9 NAS

. . . the word of God, that is, the mystery which has been hidden from the past ages and generations; but has now been manifested to His saints, to whom God willed to make known what is the riches of the glory of this mystery among the Gentiles, which is Christ in you, the hope of glory.
Colossians 1:25-27 NAS

that their hearts may be encouraged, having been knit together in love, and attaining to all the wealth that comes from the full assurance of understanding, resulting in a true knowledge of God's mystery, that is, Christ Himself, in whom are hidden all the treasures of wisdom and knowledge. Colossians 2:2-3 NAS

Here it is, the Word of God was in a mystery that was hidden and now is revealed. This mystery is about Christ and His work in and through His people and that is the hope of glory.

When Jesus and His disciples thought about the Old Testament scriptures, they believed that the scriptures pointed to Christ and His work. That is to say they believed one must view the scriptures from a "Christo-centric" viewpoint.

And behold, two of them were going that very day to a village named Emmaus, which was about seven miles from Jerusalem. And they were conversing with each other about all these things which had taken place. And it came about that while they were conversing and discussing, Jesus Himself approached, and began traveling with them. Luke 24:13-16 NAS

And beginning with Moses and with all the prophets, He explained to them the things concerning Himself in all the Scriptures. Luke 24:27 NAS

And they said to one another, "Were not our hearts burning within us while He was speaking to us on the road, while He was explaining the Scriptures to us?" Luke 24:32 NAS

And the eunuch answered Philip and said, "Please tell me, of whom does the prophet say this? Of himself, or of someone else?" And Philip opened his mouth, and beginning from this Scripture he preached Jesus to him. Acts 8:34-35 NAS

It is evident that Jesus and His disciples are interpreting the Old Testament in the light of the mystery. They believe that the

Holy Spirit is really speaking of Christ and His work in and through His people. The book of Leviticus must be about this Theme, and if we do not find it, we will have failed in our study of the Book.

Assumptions

I assume that the scripture is supernatural in nature and is the Word of God, the final authority for life and behavior, and God's Self-revelation. Therefore, I assume that Moses is its human author as the scriptures testify. All discussion of authorship is polemic and the authorship of Moses is only brought in question by the theological school who perceive the scripture to be a human document and subject only to the same hermeneutical scrutiny as all human productions. That hermeneutical methodology attempts to account for the data of scripture apart from the supernatural. Hence, problems that are resolved with a supernatural explanation are considered invalid by these theologians. Since I am not writing to convince them, I will not waste time or space with that type of documentation. Those questions are valid and many have addressed them.

Leviticus

This book, more than any other, is a theological treatise on *holiness*. Leviticus discusses the issues of man's sinfulness and God's holiness. It addresses the topic of God's solution to man's sin. It also defines that which qualifies a person for dwelling in God's presence. In these lessons some of this material will be extracted and the theological principles will be brought over into our time and applied to our lives.

Outline

The Book may be divided as follows (Outline developed by J. Sidlow Baxter 1973, p. 152)

I.   The Ground of Fellowship—Sacrifice   (1-17)
    A.   The Offerings (Absolution)   (1-7)
    B.   The Priesthood(Mediation)   (8-10)
    C.   The People (Purification)   (11-16)
    D.   The Altar (reconciliation)   (17)

II.   The Walk of Fellowship—Separation   (18-27)
    A.   Regulations Concerning the People   (18-20)
    B.   Regulations Concerning the Priest   (21-22)
    C.   Regulations Concerning the Feasts & etc. (23-24)
    D.   Regulations Concerning Canaan   (25-27)

Lesson Format

Each Lesson in Leviticus the student will find the following components:

- Pre-session Assignment

  The pre-session assignment will contain questions about the section in Leviticus that will be discussed in the next lesson. These questions will help prepare the student to understand the discussion and will guide his reading and thinking about the text.

- Class Discussion Guide

  The lesson guide and book is designed for making notes of the lecture and or discussion. It will also be an aid for further study and help the student recall materials discussed. Some students may use the resource as a distance learning resource. Make sure to do the pre-session assignment before attempting the lesson.

  A glossary of words and terms is provided on pages 66 and 67 to aid the student in clarifying the studies.

Pre-Session Assignment for Lesson 1

The Offerings (1-7)

1. How many different types of offerings (sacrifices) are there and what are their names?
   Lev. 1:6, 8-13; Lev. 2:6, 14-23; Lev. 3; Lev. 4; Lev 5:14-6:7

2. What is the special phrase used to describe the offerings known as the Burnt offering, Grain (meat) offering, and the Peace (Fellowship) offering? Lev. 1:17; Lev. 2:9; Lev. 3:5

3. What is the special phrase that marks the offerings known as the Sin offering and the Trespass (Guilt) offering? Lev. 4:20, 26, 31, 35:
   Lev. 5:13, 16, 18; Lev. 6:7

4. What is the only kind of sin that a sacrifice could be made for?
   Lev. 4:2, 27; Lev. 5:15

5. Define what is meant by a "sin of ignorance (or unintentional sin)." Lev. 6:1-7. What is the word used to describe another type of sin? Num. 15:30.

6. Define the following phrase or words:
   1. The unpardonable sin (Mark 3:28, 29)
   2. Willful sin (Heb. 10:26, 27)

7. What does the New Testament say about these offerings as to sin?
   Heb. 10:1-7

8. What purpose did these offerings serve?
   Heb 9:18-23

9. Did the sin offering take into account the economic circumstances of the offerer? Lev. 4:1-5:13

10. Did the guilt offering make allowances for the financial condition of the offerer? Lev. 5:14-6:7

LESSON 1: The Offerings
Leviticus 1-7

FIVE OFFERINGS

"Offering" usually translates the Hebrew *qorban* (kor-BAWN, corban) (cp. Mark 7:11) and denotes a sacrificial gift or that which is offered. The type of offering is indicated by words that modify offering: such as, burnt, grain, peace (fellowship), sin, and trespass or guilt.

1. The Burnt Offering (Leviticus 1; 6:8-13; Numbers 28:3-15)

Hebrew = *'olah* (oh-LAH) that which ascends, wholly goes up, that is, totally consumed by fire. The Greek translates with the word *holocausta* or in the English "holocaust." It is most often translated "whole burnt offering."

The offerer provided this sacrifice as a **voluntary act of worship**. All of the sacrifice was burned (except the hide) and none was returned to the offerer. The hide was given to the priest.

The procedure for the Burnt Offering is as follows.
1. Offerer presented offering at door or entrance to courtyard.
2. Offerer laid hands on the head of the animal.
3. He killed animal by slitting the throat.
4. The priest catches and sprinkles the blood around the altar.
5. The priest cut carcass in pieces.
6. Laid on altar and all consumed.
7. Ashes removed and carried by priest outside the camp.
8. Hide given to the priest.
9. Provided a pleasant odor (sweet smell) to the Lord.

Acceptable offerings ranged from a steer to a young pigeon so that even those of poorest circumstances could participate. Only male animals were acceptable. There was a continuous succession of this offering, both public and private, so that the fire was kept burning (Leviticus 6:8, 12, 13).

The priests were to dispose of the ashes by gathering them beside the altar, and then carrying them to a clean place outside the camp (cf. Leviticus 6:10, 11). The priest was to wear his linen clothing while gathering the ashes, but was to change his clothing to carry the ashes away. The linen garments were not washed when soiled. They were discarded, ripped apart, and made into wicks for the lamps in the Holy Place.

2. The Grain (Meat, KJV) Offering (Leviticus 2; 6:14-23; 7:9-10; Numbers 15:4; 28:5)

The combined Hebrew words *minchah qorban* (min-KHAW kor-BAWN) suggest a worship offering or a sacrificial offering. Because food is being offered, different versions translate as grain, meat, meal, or cereal offering.

The offerer provided this sacrifice as a **voluntary means of providing for the priests.** A token portion was burned; the balance not burned was given to the priest (exception: the priest's personal offering in which case all was burned).

The procedure for the Grain Offering is as follows.
1. A handful of the flour, oil, and all incense were burned.
2. A priest received the remainder.
3. The offering could be…
   a. Baked in an oven.
   b. Cooked on a griddle.
   c. Cooked in a pan (probably of ceramic composition).
4. It normally was accompanied by the fellowship or peace offering.
5. It provided bread for the priests, who were required to eat it in the courtyard of the tabernacle.
6. This offering was a sweet aroma pleasing to the Lord.

3. The Fellowship (Peace – KJV) Offering (Leviticus 3; 7:11-34; 17:1-9; 19:5-8)

The Hebrew word here is *shelem* from *shalom*, "peace." It was a sacrifice of thanks or of friendship and peace and expressed a sense of well-being, harmony or fellowship.

It was brought by the worshiper as a **voluntary means to provide for thankfulness, deliverance, or blessing.** Some inner parts of the sacrificial victim were burned, but a portion was returned to the worshiper to eat. Thus, it is the only offering the offerer could participate in consumption of the offering. All of the meat had to be eaten on the day offered or on the next day.

The kidneys and its fat, the fatty tail, the liver covering (possibly the gall bladder, or liver lobe) were to be burned before the Lord. The offerer was to "wave the breast before the Lord as a wave offering." (Lev. 7:30). The wave and the heave offerings were rituals that were included in other offerings: the distinction being the direction of the motion. In the wave offering the hands move from side to side (← 🖐 →) and in the heave offering the hands move up and down (↕ 🖐 ↕).

The procedure for the Fellowship Offering is as follows.
1. The offering presented for sacrifice.
2. He laid his hands on its head.
3. He killed the sacrifice.
4. The priest sprinkled or splashed the blood against the altar.
5. The fat was burned.
6. The breast and right thigh was given to the priest.
7. The other meat was returned to offerer and spoke of fellowship between worshiper and God.
8. The offering was a sweet aroma pleasing to God.

4.   The Sin Offering (Leviticus 4:1- 5:13; 6:24-30)

The sin (Hebrew is *chatta'th*, kat-TAWTh) offering served to provide atonement for sin through the shedding of the blood of a sacrifice. The *chatta'th* means a sin, trespass, offence, fault, state of guilt, and comes from a root "to miss the mark." It was prescribed as a means to achieve atonement.

God is specific about what qualifies the sinner for this offering: the sin must have been unintentional (Leviticus 4:2) or inadvertent (Leviticus 5:1-5). The KJV uses the term "a sin of ignorance." There was no sacrifice for a highhanded sin or the action of deep rebellious self-will (Numbers 15:30). Those sinners were to be killed. Further discussion of this subject occurs at the end of this lesson.

A quote from the commentators Keil and Delitzsch is instructive concerning the distinction draw between these two types of sins. These comments are drawn from their *Commentary on the Old Testament* in its New Updated Edition, Electronic Database.

Lev 4:2 *"If a soul sin in wandering from any (mikol (OT:3605) in a partitive sense) of the commandments of Jehovah, which ought not to be done, and do any one of them" (mee'achat (OT:259) with min (OT:4480) partitive, cf. vv. 13, 22, 27, lit., anything of one). This sentence, which stands at the head of the laws for the sin-offerings, shows that the sin-offerings did not relate to sin or sinfulness in general, but to particular manifestations of sin, to certain distinct actions performed by individuals, or by the whole congregation. The distinguishing characteristic of the sin is expressed by the term bish\gaagaah (OT:7684) (in error). No sins but those committed bish\gaagaah (OT:7684) could be expiated by sin-offerings; whilst those committed with a high hand were to be punished by the extermination of the sinner (Num 15:27-31). sh\gaagaah (OT:7684), from shaagag (OT:7683) = shaagaah (OT:7686) to wander or go wrong, signifies mistake, error, oversight. But sinning "in error" is not merely sinning through ignorance (vv. 13, 22, 27, Lev 5:18), hurry, want of consideration, or carelessness (Lev 5:1,4,15), but also sinning unintentionally (Num 35:11,15,22-23);* **hence all such sins as spring from the weakness of flesh and blood, as distinguished from sins committed with a high (elevated) hand, or in haughty, defiant rebellion against God and His commandments** (1996)**.**

An important aspect of the sin offering was the use of the blood of the sin offering. On the Day of Atonement some was sprinkled before the Ark of the Covenant in the Most Holy Place. In other important cases blood was sprinkled in the Holy Place, before the veil, and smeared on the horns of the altar of incense. In lesser cases the priest was to smear some on the horns of the brazen altar, sprinkle some on the sides of that altar, and pour the remainder at the altar's base.

The procedure of the Sin Offering is as follows.
1. An Israelite presented the offering. One's circumstances dictated what was to be offered: bull, goat, lamb, 2 doves, 2 pigeons, or flour.
2. Offerer's hands were laid on head of the sacrifice.
3. The sacrifice was slain.
4. The priest sprinkled the blood.
5. Some inner parts (i.e., fat, etc) burned on altar. The sin offering of the priest and that of the whole congregation were given wholly to the Lord and the remainder of the animal was burned outside the camp. In the offerings of individuals the remainder of the animal was to be eaten by the priest in the outer court (Leviticus 6:26, 29).

6. The key phrase concerning the sin offering is that the sins will "be forgiven" (Leviticus 4:20, 26, 31, 35; 5:10, 13).
7. It was never said to be a sweet aroma to God.

5. <u>The Guilt (Trespass – KJV) Offering</u> (Leviticus 5:14-6:7; 7:1-7)

The Hebrew for this offering is *'asham* (as-SHAWM) and means guilt, fault, sin, trespass, offence, and includes compensation for these. It was prescribed in case of guilt, when holy things were violated, and when restitution could have been made. It was associated particularly with faulty religious and worship practices. It also was used when a person trespassed against a neighbor.

Only a ram without defect could be used (except in case of the leper and then a lamb was required), and there were no considerations for the financial condition of the offerer. Restitution was required to be paid to the one offended by adding 1/5 or 20% to the value of whatever damages were determined.

The procedure of the Guilt Offering is the same as the burnt offering, with the exception that only the fat and choice inner parts were burned on the altar. The remainder of the offering was either burned outside the camp or eaten by the priests.

The five offerings specified in the Law may be classified as in the following chart.

THE FIVE OFFERINGS	
<u>Compulsory</u>	<u>Voluntary</u>
Sin Guilt (Trespass)	Burnt Grain (Meat) Peace (Fellowship)
"they shall be forgiven him"	"a sweet aroma to the Lord"

Clarification of the distinction of the two types of sin may be helpful. In order for atonement to be made the offense must be a sin of ignorance (Leviticus 5:16, 18; 6:7). What is a "sin of ignorance" or "unintentional sin?" Sacrifice could only made

NOTES

for these types of sins whether it be by either the sin or guilt offering. There is no sacrifice provided for any other type of sin. We must allow the scriptures to define the terms for us. Leviticus 6:1-7 is instructive here. It tells us what to do in very specific cases of sins of trespass (guilt).

> *Then the LORD spoke to Moses, saying, "When a person sins and acts unfaithfully against the LORD, and deceives his companion in regard to a deposit or a security entrusted to him, or through robbery, or if he has extorted from his companion, or has found what was lost and lied about it and sworn falsely, so that he sins in regard to any one of the things a man may do; then it shall be, **when he sins and becomes guilty**, that he shall restore what he took by robbery, or what he got by extortion, or the deposit which was entrusted to him, or the lost thing which he found, or anything about which he swore falsely; he shall make restitution for it in full, and add to it one-fifth more. He shall give it to the one to whom it belongs on the day he presents his guilt offering. Then he shall bring to the priest his guilt offering to the LORD, a ram without defect from the flock, according to your valuation, for a guilt offering, and the priest shall make atonement for him before the LORD; and he shall be forgiven for any one of the things which he may have done to incur guilt. "*NAS

Clearly this person knows what he has done and yet he is instructed to make a guilt offering. The key is found in the phrase, ". . . and becomes guilty." In the Old Testament the person was not indwelt by the Holy Spirit and thus did not have the advantage of His convicting power. He would be confronted by others as in the case of David's sin with Bathsheba. In the New Testament the believer is indwelt by the Holy Spirit and He convicts the person of sin.

When the Spirit convicts the person about his sin, he is then confronted with the choice about whose will shall be done. When a person refuses to submit to God's will it is proof that his sin is a highhanded (defiant) sin and God cannot deal with such a sin. If one will not accept God's way, there is no other way. This is the unpardonable sin of the Gospels and the willful sin of the Book of Hebrews.

There is always a way out of sin, but one must decide to do things God's way to find it.

Pre-Session Assignment for Lesson 2

The Priesthood (Leviticus 8-10)

1. How important to God do you think is this anointing of the priest (importance implied by the number of people invited to view it)?
   (Lev. 8:1-5)

2. What three rituals did Moses perform when consecrating Aaron and his sons? (Lev. 8:6-13)

3. What else did Moses consecrate at this time and why do you feel this was necessary? (Lev. 8:10,11)

4. What was the first offering presented and for whom was it given?
   (Lev. 8:14-17)

5. Describe what was done with the blood, what was burnt on the altar, and what happened to the remainder of the animal?
   (Lev. 8:14-17)

6. What was the second offering? (Lev. 8:18-21)

7. What was the third offering? (Lev. 8:22)
   What was its special name? (Lev. 8:22)
   Describe the special blood ritual of this offering. (Lev. 8:23, 24)

8. What did Moses put in the hands of Aaron and his sons?
   (Lev. 8:27)

9. How long did the ritual of ordination last and where were they to stay during this time? (Lev. 8:33-35)

10. On the eighth day Aaron and his sons were to begin their priestly ministry. What is another ritual in which the eighth day is important to the people of Israel? (Gen. 17:12)

11. What is another important reason God would want so many people viewing the ceremonies of the time of the consecration of the priests? (Lev. 9:2-7, 24)

12. When Aaron performed this sacrifice, he was saying something very important to the people, what was it? (Lev. 9:23; Num. 6:22-27)

13. What are the names of Aaron's two oldest sons? (Lev. 10:1)

14. God kills these sons for offering something to the Lord that was not according to the Lord's will. They were consumed in a manner similar to the sacrifice itself (cf. Lev. 10:1-2 with Lev. 9:24). What did Moses say they had done by their actions? (Lev. 10:3)

15. Why do you think Aaron and his other sons were forbidden to show public sorrow for these deaths? (Lev. 10:5-7)

16. What other behavior does he warn them about? (Lev. 10:8-15)

LESSON 2: The Priesthood
Leviticus 8-10

PRIESTHOOD

Since a primary characteristic about God is His holiness, it is of absolute importance to understand that for Him to relate to people something must be done about their sinfulness and a provision must be made for a way that they could live in a manner that is consistent with His holiness (Heb 12:14 *Follow peace with all men, and holiness, without which no man shall see the Lord* KJV). For this reason this Book, a manual on holiness, begins by addressing the means of reconciling sinful man to this holy God through sacrifices and the shedding of a substitute's blood. The core of the Mosaic and the New Covenant is the sacrifice. This is of prime importance for study of Leviticus.

In order that these sacrifices be holy or that they be done in a way consistent with God's requirements, there must be someone(s) set apart (sanctified or made holy) whose responsibility is to oversee the sacrifices or to mediate on behalf of the worshipper. God appointed the first man and woman to be His priests, and it was His intention that all could be priests to Him, thereby all could mediate worship. However, man's disobedience and resulting sin meant that mediation of worship would include a work of reconciliation for the priest himself and others he represented. At first the men of the family were the priests (as indicated by the sacrifices offered by Cain and Able in Genesis 4:1-8). Later, in the days of Job and Abraham, the priesthood was invested in the patriarch (chief leader of the family group or clan). God intended that the firstborn male of each Israelite family be a priest (Exodus 13:1, 2, 11-13; 19:6, 21, 24). The replacement of the firstborn with the Levites is found in Numbers 3:44-48. It appears that the loyalty of the Levites to the covenant at the time of the golden calf incident (Exodus 32:26-28) led God to give the privilege of mediating worship to them.

A new priesthood arises in the new covenant, the high priesthood of Jesus Christ (priesthood after the order of Melchizedek). He will remain the High Priest forever to mediate for all men. He also establishes a new "holy" people, a kingdom of priests (Revelation 1:6). This is the priesthood in which all believers can mediate worship before God.

This section of Leviticus (8-10) illustrates how important God feels about worship being holy; that is, done according to God's prescription. We see how Aaron and the Levites get their start. It was an awesome occasion and meant to impress those who observed it. In the ritual they were:

- Presented to the people at the gate of the tabernacle.
- Washed.
- Clothed in their spectacular clothing.
- Anointed.
- Atoned by sacrifice.

An illustration of the garments of the high priest follows.

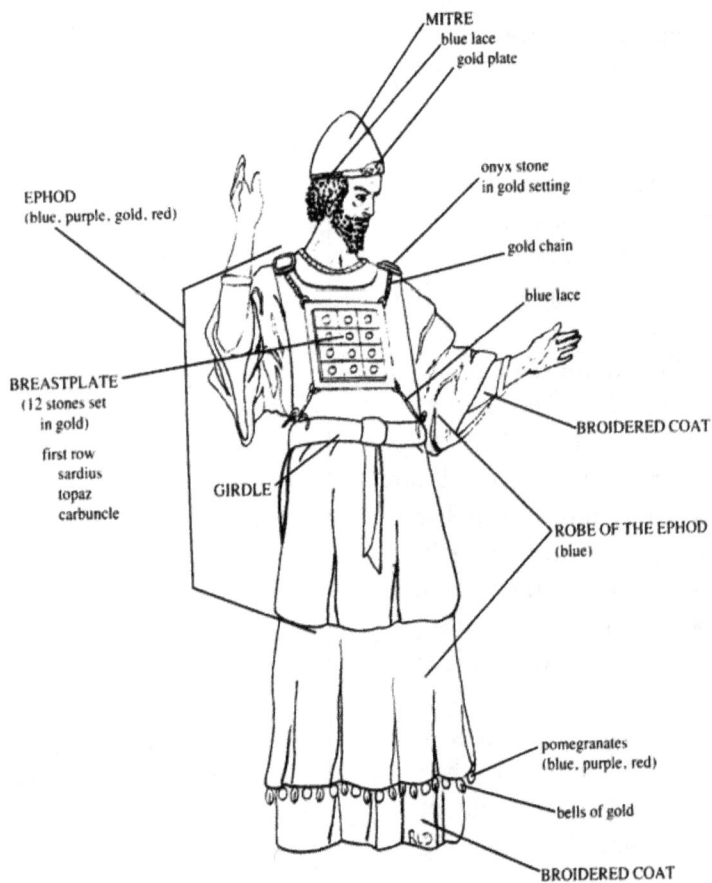

MITRE
blue lace
gold plate

onyx stone
in gold setting

gold chain

blue lace

EPHOD
(blue, purple, gold, red)

BREASTPLATE
(12 stones set
in gold)

first row
sardius
topaz
carbuncle

GIRDLE

BROIDERED COAT

ROBE OF THE EPHOD
(blue)

pomegranates
(blue, purple, red)

bells of gold

BROIDERED COAT

Figure 1: The High Priest[2]

[2] Drawing by Dewitt 1988, p. 96

The only other clothing the priest wore (not shown here) were his undergarments—linen britches and linen undershirt. The priest wore no shoes while carrying out his duties of worship. Whenever a person in the Old Testament drew near to the Lord, he was told to remove his shoes. This may have been the custom upon entering a home. It shows respect for the person and his/her home and is a way of showing respect for the presence of the Lord and humility when around Him. Sometimes shoes were removed when certifying a covenant as in the case of Boaz in the Book of Ruth. In the New Testament there may be some relationship to foot washing.

Once the priest was washed and clothed, it was time to ordain him and honor his consecration. This ritual involved anointing with oil. The anointing involves pouring or smearing oil on the person and in this case it was pouring as recorded in:

A Song of Ascents, of David. Behold, how good and how
*   pleasant it is for brothers to dwell together in unity!*
It is like the precious oil upon the head, coming down upon the
*   beard, even Aaron's beard, coming down upon the edge of*
*   his robes.* Ps 133:1-2 NAS

NOTES

Figure 2: Moses anoints Aaron with oil[3]

---
[3] Drawing by DeWitt 1988, p. 85

Not only were the priests anointed but so was the Tabernacle and its furniture. The ritual of this ordination lasted over a period of 7 days and on the 8th day (8 is the number of new beginnings) they began their ministry. All seven days included sacrifices for these who were to be the priests.

The Hebrew word translated "ordain" literally means to "fill the hands." So when one is ordained his hands are filled with the task. He is set apart (holy) to this work.

ORDINATION AND OFFERINGS

For the priests to properly mediate the sacrifices for others they themselves had to be in right (holy) relationship with God. Therefore, several offerings were prescribed:
1. A bull for a sin offering.
2. A ram for a burnt offering.
3. The ram of consecration or filling—a special peace offering.
    *   A filling because parts of this sacrifice was placed in their hands to wave before the Lord as a wave offering.
    *   Blood of this sacrifice was applied to their right ear, right thumb, and right big toe.
4. These rituals and offerings were duplicated for the next six days while they remained in the court of the tabernacle.

On the 8th day Aaron and his sons began their ministry and the Lord confirmed the work by sending heavenly fire to consume the sacrifices.

STRANGE FIRE AND DEATH

The oldest boys of Aaron, Nadab and Abihu, showed irreverence and disrespect for the holy by offering incense with a strange or unauthorized fire. What this strange fire was we are not informed, but it is sufficient to be told it was a failure to honor God as holy. Holiness is about a relation-ship in which God as our owner has the right to spell out the policy regarding the use or operation of any thing. Rebellion, disobedience or refusal to follow God's prescriptions results in death. The result of the misuse of the holy will always be deadly. There are people who attend church regularly and yet they are spiritually dead or dying. They have no victory, no
joy, no peace and wonder why their Christian experience is so

LEVITICUS
Page 25

empty. Perhaps they should review their response to God's will.

The other family members (father and brothers) were to give no indication of grief. Their body language was to maintain a clear message that no one approved the actions of those who disregarded the God of covenant. Mediation of worship is a serious business. We should never treat our praise time in an insincere manner (i.e., as familiar or flippant). Whatever we do we are to do as to the Lord. We are to do so wholeheartedly by putting our strength, energy and whole mind into it.

NOTES

Pre-Session Assignment for Lesson 3

The People Part I (11, 12, & 15)

Distinction of the Clean and Unclean—FOODS.
Remember that the real message is about what goes into the heart. Rules for foods are in 4 categories: animals, fish, fowl, and insects.

Animals (11:1-8)
    1.
    2.

Fish (11:9-12)
    1.
    2.

Fowl or Birds (11:13-19)
    1.
    2.
    3.

Insects (11:20-23)
    1.
    2.
    3.

Defilement or contact with the body of an unclean creature (11:24-40)
    1.
    2.
    3.

The New Testament makes it clear that these foods do not defile the person, but in a New Testament sense one may be defiled.
1. What does Jesus pronounce? (example: Matt. 15:10-19)

2. Hebrews 12:15 tells something that defiles.

3. James 3:6 tells of a small thing that defiles.

Lev. 12 contains rules about childbirth. What do these rules imply about the sinfulness of the human race?

Lev. 15 speaks to defilement as a result of bodily discharges, make a list of as many of these types of defilement as you can find.

Leviticus has described three stages of uncleanness and prescribes for its removal in each case. Can you find them?

LESSON 3: The People, Part I
Leviticus 11, 12, 15

FOODS

The Holy God began this book on relationship by providing the means so that man and He might relate to one another. The basis of that relation-ship is sacrifice (substitute by blood). In order for this worship to occur in proper order a priest must mediate. So, our second lesson was about the priesthood. Now the book turns its attention to issues that affect the relationship that has been established through blood sacrifice. These are things that can contaminate the purity or holiness of the fellowship and render the person unfit (unclean) for the presence of God. In fact, the bulk of this book speaks to this issue.

It is fitting that the first area to be discussed is contamination from ingestion of forbidden (unclean) foods and touching unclean objects. Most of the defilements in today's lesson issue from within the person.

The instructions are normally easier to remember when thinking about what is allowed rather than what is forbidden. Four groups of foods are categorized:
1. Animals that are allowed to be eaten are:
    a. Split the hooves (two-toed)
    b. Chew the cud

2. Fish considered as clean food must have:
    a. Scales
    b. Fins

3. Insects allowed to be eaten must be among the following kinds:
    a. Jointed hind legs for jumping or hopping
    b. These eat fresh grains and grasses

4. Birds, unlike the other categories of food, are best distinguished by those which are forbidden for consumption.
    a. Carnivorous birds (meat eaters)
    b. Carrion-eaters (road-kill scavengers)
    c. Predacious birds (hunters for meat)

These foods contributed to good health, but this does not seem to be the emphasis given in this chapter. They are linked twice in the chapter (11:44, 45) to the statement "I am holy."

The New Testament makes it clear that physical foods were never God's intention when He spoke of defilement. Remember defilement is a spiritual message to be received by people having the Spirit to interpret it. God speaks to the Old Testament people about the physical because that is the only level on which He could communicate with them. However, the following verses make clear the intent of the Lord.

And He said to them, "Are you so lacking in understanding also? Do you not understand that whatever goes into the man from outside cannot defile him; because it does not go into his heart, but into his stomach, and is eliminated? "(Thus He declared all foods clean.) And He was saying, "That which proceeds out of the man, that is what defiles the man. "For from within, out of the heart of men, proceed the evil thoughts, fornications, thefts, murders, adulteries, deeds of coveting and wickedness, as well as deceit, sensuality, envy, slander, pride and foolishness. "All these evil things proceed from within and defile the man." Mark 7:17-23 NAS

And Peter answered and said to Him, "Explain the parable to us." And He said, "Are you still lacking in understanding also? "Do you not understand that everything that goes into the mouth passes into the stomach, and is eliminated? "But the things that proceed out of the mouth come from the heart, and those defile the man.
Matt 15:15-18 NAS

Jesus explains that foods could not actually defile the person because God designed the body to eliminate them. The play on words could not be plainer. It is not that which goes into the mouth that defiles, but things that come out of the mouth can defile because they proceed from the heart. The focus changes from the stomach and the alimentary canal to the heart and what it ingests.

That men would not catch this change is clear from the writing of Paul. Those who impose this part of the law on the person is said to be "giving heed to seducing spirits and doctrines [*teachings*] of demons.

Now the Spirit speaketh expressly, that in the latter times some shall depart from the faith, giving heed to seducing spirits, and doctrines of devils; speaking lies in hypocrisy; having their conscience seared with a hot iron; forbidding to marry, and **commanding to abstain from meats, which God hath created to be received with thanksgiving of them which believe and know the truth. For every creature of God is good, and nothing to be refused,** *if it be received with thanksgiving: for it is sanctified by the word of God and prayer.* 1 Tim 4:1-5 KJV

It is important that we understand the concepts of defilement and unclean-ness. Defilement (contamination) occurs when one violates the policies (rules) about what one may touch, taste, or do. The word contamination suggests that something has been corrupted. Corruption is the word used in the New Testament to describe the consequences of sin and/or the flesh (Romans 8:21; Galatians 6:8; 2 Peter 1:4; 2:19).

The following reference in 2 Peter is interesting:
For speaking out arrogant words of vanity they entice by fleshly desires, by sensuality, those who barely escape from the ones who live in error, promising them freedom while they themselves are **slaves of corruption***; for by what a man is overcome, by this he is enslaved. For if after they have escaped* **the defilements of the world** *by the knowledge of the Lord and Savior Jesus Christ, they are again entangled in them and are overcome, the last state has become worse for them than the first. For it would be better for them not to have known the way of righteousness, than having known it, to turn away from the holy commandment delivered to them.* 2 Peter 2:18-21 NAS

Peter speaks of the defilements of the world that they had escaped only to become entangled again and arrive at a cruel end.

Defilement renders the person unclean (a state in which one is unfit to enter the presence of God or draw near to God). Demons in the Synoptic Gospels are consistently referred to as "unclean spirits." When a New Covenant believer defiles himself and becomes unclean the following things may be evidences.

- A tendency to withdraw from the fellowship of the believers.
- He may have feelings of alienation from God.
- He may manifest disinterest in prayer, praise and Bible study.
- He may hold resentment toward leaders and other Christians.

How does one ingest unclean things into his heart so that it defiles him? The Scriptures warn us about the thoughts and beliefs one may entertain.
For as he thinks within himself, so he is. Proverbs 23:7 NAS

For the word of God is living and active and sharper than any two-edged sword, and piercing as far as the division of soul and spirit, of both joints and marrow, and able to judge the thoughts and intentions of the heart. Hebrews 4:12-13 NAS

And do not be conformed to this world, but be transformed by the renewing of your mind, that you may prove what the will of God is, that which is good and acceptable and perfect. Romans 12:2 NAS

Finally, brethren, whatever is true, whatever is honorable, whatever is right, whatever is pure, whatever is lovely, whatever is of good repute, if there is any excellence and if anything worthy of praise, let your mind dwell on these things. Philippians 4:8 NAS

What one sees, hears and meditates on will determine what will come out of the heart through the mouth to either profit or defile that one. There is some music that is unclean. There are movies and reading material that are unclean. There is rumor and gossip that is unclean and will lead to one's defilement just as surly as eating pork would have done so for the Israelite.

Stop now, evaluate the type of thoughts you have been entertaining.

Chapters 12 and 15 continue this theme. Chapter 12 provides for a period of uncleanness for a mother following the birth of a child. The picture confirms that all humans are born in sin. Sin entered the human race through our father Adam.

One reason for the longer period of defilement following the birth of a daughter may have been a way of increasing a sense of value of female children.

Chapter 15 deals with emissions of body fluids. These include seminal emissions (male) and the menstrual flow (female). Because these relate to birth and blood, both are considered as a source of defilement. One might also understand how these laws provide for good hygiene, sanitation, and disease control. The following is an outline of chapter 15:

A_1. Male abnormal emissions (2-15)

    B_1. Male normal emissions (16-18)

    B_2. Female normal emissions (19-24)

A_2. Female abnormal emissions (25-20)

THREE STATES OF UNCLEANNESS

1. That which defiled until evening (e.g., touching a dead animal). A person was to bathe and wash his clothes
2. That which defiled for 7 days (e.g., touching a human corpse). The cleansing ritual involved a simple ceremony such as a sacrifice of two birds or being sprinkled with water of cleansing.
3. That which defiled indefinitely (e.g., leprosy). The cleansing depended upon removal of the cause of the uncleanness, followed by a formal ceremony.

Pre-Session Assignment for Lesson 4

The People Part II (Lev. 13, 14)
"The Law of the Leper"

1. What is the total number of occurrences of the phrases, "show it to the priest," or "the priest shall look upon it," or "the priest shall see it?"

2. If leprosy symbolizes sin, what would an "infection of leprosy" represent? (or infectious skin disease, or leprous sore, etc)

3. Is this chapter primarily concerned with those who had been leprous or with those who became leprous as they traveled?

4. As you read this chapter, who do you feel is responsible to discover and reveal spots on the skin when they occur?

5. According to Lev. 13:3 what is the first "sign" the priest is to observe in order to know if the infection is leprous?

6. In the verse mentioned (question 5) what was the second sign the priest was to find in order to identify the infection as leprous?

7. What was the priest to do if he was not sure the spot was leprosy? (Lev. 13:4-8)

8. What does the priest know if the flesh around the mark was raw? (Lev. 13:10, 11)

9. If the priest pronounced the person to be leprous, what was the person required to declare about himself? (Lev. 13:45)

10. What is the person saying about himself when he makes the declaration in question 9?

11. What other action must the leper be willing to do? (Lev. 13:46)

12. How would the people know when a person was to be restored from his infection? (Lev. 14:2, 3)

13. How many birds were used in the cleansing ceremony for the leper and why were there more than one? (Lev. 14:4-11)

14. What did the priest do with some of the blood of the guilt offering? (Lev. 14:14)

15. Restoration also required the priest to use anointing oil: in what way did he use it? (Lev. 14:17, 18)

16. Why do you think that such an elaborate ceremony was needed for the cleansing of leprosy?

NOTES

LESSON 4 The People Part II (Leviticus 13, 14)
"The Law of the Leper"

The instructions given in these two chapters are extremely important to the life of the community of believers. No condition was more frightening to the people of the Old Testament era than leprosy. It was so contagious that it could decimate whole populations. It was a hideous disease to behold as it consumed the person while alive. It was indeed a living death.

The infections called leprosy here in these chapters is a type (symbolic of) the infection of sin. Sin is like leprosy in that it is a living death and ends in death. It is highly contagious to the community of believers. God has given clear pictures of the swift action needed to confront sin in the stories of Achan in the book of Joshua and of Ananias and Sapphira in Acts.

These two chapters (Leviticus 13, 14) were written to inform Israel of the process of removing the uncleanness of leprosy and restoring the leper when new cases of infection were identified. It helped them to identify chronic or recurring cases. It is for us a picture of how the church is to deal with cases of sin infections that occur among saints.

 MODELS FOR ACCOUNTABILITY AND RESTORATION OF BELIEVERS

This is the only passage I know of in the Bible that gives explicit and implicit instructions for personal accountability and for restoration of those who have been taken by a sin infection.

MODEL FOR ACCOUNTABILITY RELATIONSHIPS

The phrases "the priest shall look at the mark" or "the priest shall see it" occur at least 27 times in chapter 13. The Israelite is instructed that when a mark occurs on his body, he is to show it to the priest. At this point no one has confirmed that the spot is leprosy. It is just a spot at the moment. The individual is to take the initiative to go show it to the priest for evaluation. Note the following insights for accountability type of relationships.

- All need to be aware that spots can and do develop.
- Accountability can only happen when people are in a community relationship.
- Accountability is a voluntary action, not one that is coerced.
- Each person must take the initiative to risk exposure and quarantine. It is not the responsibility of the priest to search for spots.
- For this kind of relationship to work one must "buy into" the concept that God's people DO NOT exist outside of the context of community. Being a connected part of a local church is not about doing religious things; it is about being part of a family where the family's well-being is of vital concern.

Exposure of spots is the route to healing.

Is anyone among you sick? Let him call for the elders of the church, and let them pray over him, anointing him with oil in the name of the Lord; and the prayer offered in faith will restore the one who is sick, and the Lord will raise him up, and if he has committed sins, they will be forgiven him. Therefore, confess your sins to one another, and pray for one another, so that you may be healed. The effective prayer of a righteous man can accomplish much. James 5:14-16 NAS

In the New Testament all believers are priests (Revelation 1:6). I am not suggesting that the pastor and/or elders be the only one(s) to whom spots are revealed. All of us should have accountability relationships within the body of believers at the level of "friends." These are friends within the context of John 15:13-15.
"Greater love has no one than this, that one lay down his life for his friends. "You are My friends, if you do what I command you. "No longer do I call you slaves, for the slave does not know what his master is doing; but I have called you friends, for all things that I have heard from My Father I have made known to you. NAS

This is a level of relationship where there are no hidden things. One does not have many of these relationships. They happen when people are joined in heart and covenant as David and Jonathan were. This type of relationship occurs when one's desire is not for what one can receive from the relationship but for what one may give. Many desire a friend but have difficulty obtaining one because their focus is on what they think they need for themselves.

Friends do not break confidences. So, one is secure to show spots to the other person. The love of a friend covers a multitude of transgressions for his/her focus is restoration not exposure. Friends will speak the truth to one another in love. A friend does not get his feelings hurt when a friend uncovers his spots.

Due to the lack of this kind of relationship in the church, people who need to be healed are not because they do not confess their sin. The prayer of faith cannot be made, and they continue in their infections.

Sin infections may occur in any area of one's life—finances, emotions, relationships, sex, ministry, thoughts, etc. A sin infection occurs when one is drawn away by lust, is confronted by a temptation, and gives in to it. When the infection is not identified and confronted, it will infect others due to its contagious nature. The end result may be that an epidemic of sin infections decimates the community.

God's first strategy is to isolate the infected person. The purposes are to help the person heal and secondly, to prevent the spread of the infection. These sin infections are dangerous to a church community because the infection is an infection of mind, heart and mouth. The infection is spread mouth to ear. The person with the infection needs to be healed of unclean and erroneous thinking. The quarantine period is expressly to deal with these thoughts and ideas that are deep rooted and are the source of unclean behavior. Therefore, just isolating the sinner is insufficient. A "priest" should help him explore thinking and to look for the roots of the infection.

Some infections start within, as in the case of a spot associated with a boil (Leviticus 13:18-23). A boil is an infection related to the blood. Some people have let little things get into their spirit where it festers and births an infection. The one who is blamed for the pain may not know about it and does not realize that the person was offended, in fact, nothing may have occurred to wound the person. This infection is symbolized in Leviticus 13 by burns (13:24-28). These are those offenses and trespasses that have wounded the individual, have not been managed and become an infection. Whether originating from within, or without all of these should not ultimately infect the believer who is in effective accountable relationships.

RECOGNIZING LEPROSY (SIN INFECTIONS)

The priests were not expert medical personnel. You may feel that you are inadequate to help friends find healing for their spots as well. God made it very clear what the priest was to look for in order to declare the person clean or unclean (non-leprous or leprous).

"When a man has on the skin of his body a swelling or a scab or a bright spot, and it becomes an infection of leprosy on the skin of his body, then he shall be brought to Aaron the priest, or to one of his sons the priests. And the priest shall look at the mark on the skin of the body, and if the hair in the infection has turned white and the infection appears to be deeper than the skin of his body, it is an infection of leprosy; when the priest has looked at him, he shall pronounce him unclean. Leviticus 13:2-3 NAS

When the person shows the priest the spot or mark on his flesh, the priest is to look for the following:
1. Is there white hair in the mark?
   a. White hair is a sign of aging and deterioration.
   b. Ask, what do you see deteriorating in the person's life?
      i. Their prayer life.
      ii. Their Bible reading and study.
      iii. Their praise and worship.
      iv. Their church attendance.
      v. Their giving.
      vi. Their service.

2. Is the infection deeper than the surface?
   a. Does the initial probe show that the problem reaches back some distance in the history of the person?
   b. Does the examination show that the problem is in other areas of the person's life as well (e.g., lustful thoughts concerning sexual behavior may indicate a lack of control of other areas such as a greed for riches, or covetousness of things of others)?

What if the priest is having difficulty determining these things? He is to isolate the person for a specified period for

NOTES

observation (13:4-8). The period is for seven days after which the priest examines the spot. He is trying to discover whether the infection is spreading or not. If he is still unsure, he is to keep the person isolated for a second seven days. Again he is looking to see if the spot is spreading. If it is not, it is something that is getting well and the person is declared clean. If it spreads, the person is declared unclean. The symbolism indicates that at times periods of observation are needed to find out whether the infection is spreading in the person's spirit. Look to see what kind of attitude is developing.

Sometimes another symptom is observed. Besides the white skin and white hair the flesh is raw (13:10-15), and the priest is to pronounce the person unclean as it is a chronic or recurring case of infection. When there is a demonstration of the flesh (Galatians 5:19-21) and it is recurring, it is clearly a sin infection. For example, when immorality occurs (such as adultery or fornication) it is an indication that there is a history of infection that must be dealt with before cleansing can occur.

When uncleanness is declared (the infection has produced a defilement that affects the person's ability to relate to a Holy God), the steps of restoration may begin.

RESTORING THE LEPER

1. One starts recovery with a willingness to declare, "I am unclean." (13:45)
   a. It is accompanied by appropriate body language.
      i. Tearing his clothes was a cultural sign of mourning.
      ii. Hair of his head was to be uncovered which was a Jewish sign of rejection from worship.
      iii. Covering one's mustache was a sign of humility and lack of dependence on one's manhood or abilities.
   b. This demonstrates that the person has an appreciation for the effects of his sin on his relationship with God.
      i. To say "I am unclean" is to say that I have been defiled and therefore I am unfit to enter God's presence.
      ii. It meant for the Israelite that he was excluded from approaching God in the sanctuary.

    iii. It declares a clear sense of loss and results in mourning

2. Secondly, one must demonstrate a willingness to be isolated until pronounced clean (13:46).
   a. This demonstrates a clear understanding of the affect of one's sin on the community
      i. Until this occurs the infection has not been nor can be effectively purged.
      ii. Failure here will cause the leper to:
         1. See himself as the victim rather than the villain,
         2. Run from the healing process rather than embrace it,
         3. See himself as being in charge of the healing process and responsible to declare his own cleanness (a righteousness that is as filthy rags).
   b. This demonstrates an understanding of the contagious nature of one's sin on the community.
   c. This demonstrates an understanding of the lengthy nature of the healing process.

3. Thirdly, a person must develop a new appreciation of the death, burial, and resurrection of our Lord and the work of His blood in one's life (14:2-14)
   a. Two birds were used because they could not raise to life the bird which was killed. So, one bird represents the death of Christ and the other the resurrection of Christ.
   b. One bird is slain over a basin of water. The blood flows into the water. The wing and tail feathers of the living bird are fanned and dipped into the bloody water. The priest holds the bird, a red woolen string, a piece of cedar wood, and hyssop as he sprinkles the recovering leper with the bloody water symbolizing his cleansing from the defilement of his leprosy.
      i. Next the priest examines the leper.
      ii. The recovered leper severs the past by certain actions (14:9).
   c. Guilt and sin offerings were made, and some blood of the guilt offering was applied to the right ear, right thumb, and right big toe.

    i. This speaks of one's mind, one's service, and one's walk.

    ii. Shows a new appreciation for the redemptive work of Christ

4. Finally, one must receive a fresh infilling of the Holy Spirit (14:15-18).
   a. Holy anointing oil was placed over the blood on the three special locations on the body.
   b. The balance of the oil in the palm of priest was placed on head of the restored leper.
   c. A new appreciation for the work of Christ and a new anointing prepare the person to retake his/her place in the community of faith.

None of these four steps may be excused if full recovery is to be accomplished. The emphases of both of these chapters are needed to help to recover those taken in a sin. We need to identify sin infections (Leviticus 13), and we need to be able to restore the one so infected when he recovers (Leviticus 14). When the leper recovers, the church needs to make sure he is returned to his rightful place in the community.

It might be helpful to talk about the concept of isolation, as it would be applied in the church today. We would not physically put people out of the community, but we could set them away from their normal and typical routine. For example, if a person's sin infection was in their management of finances, one might be required to give a weekly report of financial management until it became apparent he had made proper changes in that area of his life. One might step aside from a position of ministry in the body until it was clear that he was morally clean in thought and deed.

All of the concepts of the Law of the Leper work from a foundation of relationships. The community of faith must establish the need for a body of believers who live relationally before the complete paradigm of The Law of the Leper will be affective. The Church is not a place where the paradigm of the "Lone Ranger" fits.

Pre-Session Assignment for Lesson 5

The Day of Atonement (16) & The Altar (17)

1. What special room in the Tabernacle was important for the Day of Atonement? (16:2, 3)

2. What garments was the high priest to wear on this occasion? (16:4 cp. 16:23, 24)

3. The bull for the sin offering was for whom? (16:3 cp. 16:6, 11)

4. The two goats (16:5) were for the sin offering of whom? (16:15)

5. Before Aaron sprinkled the blood of the bull he was to do what? (16:12, 13)

6. Why were two goats used in the offering? (16:20-22, 26)

7. What do you think the two goats symbolized?

8. When did this special Day of Atonement occur? (16:29)

9. What happens to the Israelite who does not take his offering to the Tabernacle for sacrifice? (17:5)

10. To whom were they never to sacrifice? (17:7)

11. Why were the Israelites to hold blood with special regard and not eat it? (17:10, 11)

12. How did the hunter show an appreciation for the sanctity of life? (17:13, 14)

LESSON 5 The Day of Atonement (16) & The Altar (17)
Yom Kippur

As we come to the end of Part I of the book of Leviticus we remember that this part concerns the basis of our fellowship with a holy God—sacrifice. The great divide between this God and man is caused by one thing alone—sin. Therefore, this part speaks, in large measure, to the problem of the uncleanness that sin brings upon man. It is fitting that we should end Part I by discussing the greatest day of the year in the Jewish calendar, *Yom Kippur* (Day of Atonement).

The Day of Atonement occurs in early fall, on the tenth day of the seventh month of the Jewish calendar (this is only five days before the Feast of Booths). It was a day of mourning and repentance, abstaining from secular activities, and of fasting. In fact, it was the only day in the sacred calendar that specifically prescribed fasting. Atonement affects three persons or things in this chapter: the high priest himself, the sanctuary, and the people.

Repetition of some key phrases in the 16th chapter should alert us to core ideas. Before any other thing can happen the priest must face his own sins and sinfulness. The phrase "for himself" occurs seven times in 16:6, 11, 17, and 24. The high priest can not minister on the behalf of others (mediate) until he makes atonement for his own sin.

Secondly, things as well as people need atonement on this day. So, a sin offering is made to atone for the sanctuary (note: vv. 16, 18, 19, 20, 33). Judgment against sin begins at God's house. Do not expect God to begin house cleaning with those most far from Him.

"To make atonement" is the translation of the Hebrew verb *kipper* (kee-pir), which means "to expiate" or "make atonement." Several verses from this 16th chapter are all that have survived from the Targum of Leviticus among the Dead Sea Scrolls and it translates the Hebrew *kapporet* (kap-PO-ret: mercy seat, propitiatory) using an Aramaic word meaning "cover, lid." What is interesting about the use of this verb here is how the Hebrew handles the object of the verb. In Leviticus the subject is the priest, never God. In other words, it is the priest who makes atonement. If it is for a person that the priest makes atonement, the Hebrew uses a preposition before the person. The priest makes atonement "for" or "on behalf of" the person. The person is not the object of the rite of expiation—the blood is not poured on or rubbed on him—but he is the one who benefits from the rite. In contrast, things (inanimate objects) may be the direct object of the verb *kipper*. Thus, atonement is made for people and conversely the sanctuary and altar are atoned. The implication is that the priest's acts of *kipper* are prerequisite but do not cause forgiveness, only God Himself gives forgiveness and grants atonement. Only God can open the way for man to come into relationship with the Holy God.

It is only on this day, *Yom Kipporim,* (yome kee-PO-reem) that the blood is carried into the inner sanctum of the sanctuary (the Holy of Holies). The Hebrew word for "transgressions" in 16:16, 21, conveys the idea of revolt or rebellion and indicates the worst of sin (sin in its most gross manifestation). For this reason the blood is carried as close as possible to the presence of God.

The following figure illustrates the use of the blood in the different offerings.

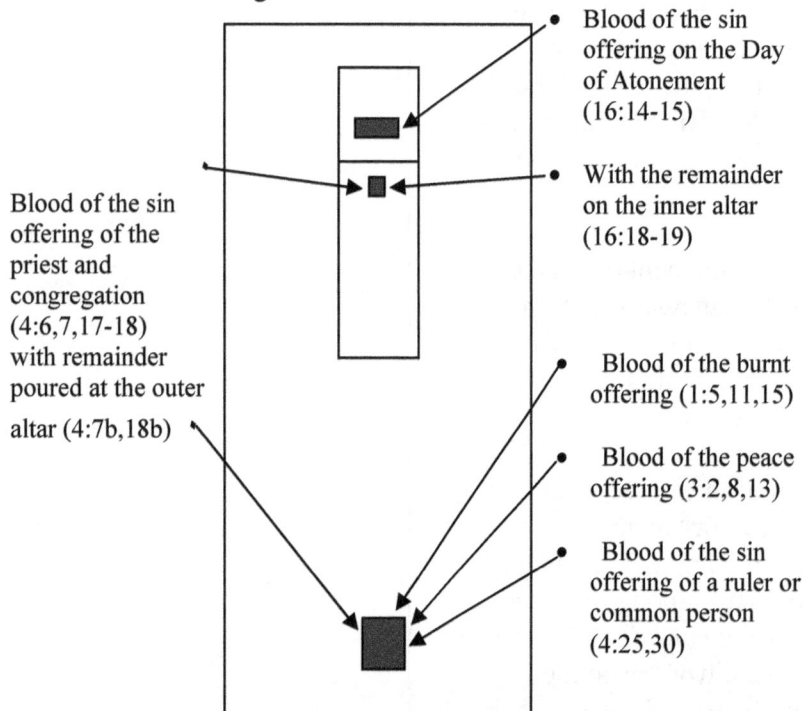

Blood of the sin offering on the Day of Atonement (16:14-15)

With the remainder on the inner altar (16:18-19)

Blood of the sin offering of the priest and congregation (4:6,7,17-18) with remainder poured at the outer altar (4:7b,18b)

Blood of the burnt offering (1:5,11,15)

Blood of the peace offering (3:2,8,13)

Blood of the sin offering of a ruler or common person (4:25,30)

Figure 3 The Application of the Blood

The procedures of the Day are as follows:

1. Aaron bathed and dressed in ordinary priestly garments.
2. He offered a bull as his own sin offering.
3. He entered the Most Holy Place with incense and then with the blood of his sin offering.
4. He made incense to envelop the mercy seat and cherubim.
5. He sprinkled the blood on the mercy seat and seven times in front of it.
6. He slew a goat for the people's sin offering and sprinkled its blood in the Most Holy Place where he had sprinkled the bull's blood.
7. He cleansed and atoned the Holy Place and its furnishings and the altar of sacrifice by sprinkling or anointing with blood.
8. He imputed the people's sins to the scapegoat and sent it away.
9. He bathed and put on his glorious garments.
10. He offered a burnt offering for himself and for the people.

THE SCAPEGOAT

The presentation of the blood of the slain sin offering was one-half of the ceremony of the Day of Atonement. The second half was unique to this day. Two goats were chosen for the ceremony and offering. Lots were cast and one goat was selected to be slain and the other to be the *azazel* (aza-zel) or "scapegoat." This word means the "gone goat" or "the goat of entire removal." After the blood of the slain goat has been presented to God Aaron laid his hands on the head of the *azazel* and confessed Israel's sins and transgressions thus imputing or transferring Israel's sins to the goat. A man from the congregation chosen by lot led the *azazel* away into the wilderness to be set free and lost there. This symbolizes the resurrection of Jesus and His bearing our sins away.

The goat "bears" the iniquities to the wilderness. The same Hebrew word that conveys the concept of "bearing or carrying" also means "to forgive."

THE ALTAR (Leviticus 17)

Scholars often refer to Leviticus 17-26 as the Holiness Code or Holiness Manifesto. The section reaffirms that God is holy and all holiness is from Him. Since holiness is a chief aspect of His character, it is to be the chief aspect of the character of the people of God.

However, we are using the chapter to close the first half of the book of Leviticus. As such, it is fitting that the section that opened with instructons about offerings would end with instructions about the place they are to be made—the brazen altar. They were not to worship by borrowing their style and method from the pagans surrounding them. Those may sacrifice and worship on any "high place," but not so for God's people. They may eat meat with the blood in it, but not the Israelite. They may offer a portion of a slaughtered animal to the goat demons of the open field to ensure new crops and well-being, but not so for the Israelite, for he is to believe that only *Yahweh* (Yah-way) provides.

So, the chapter is about the only place to put the blood of a slaughtered animal. As long as they are in the wilderness going to the promised land they were to bring clean animals to be killed to the tabernacle and give the blood and the fat to the Lord. When they enter the land this rule is altered (Deuteronomy 12:15).

This rule is to make sure that they were not turned in their hearts back to Egyptian practice where goats were worshiped much like Pan was. Pan was a goat-like demon who reresented the male and fertilizing principle in nature. The Egyptians called him *Mendes* (Men-des) and listed him as one of the eight main gods. Here was a superstition left over from their former life in Egypt.

If the Israelite killed a clean animal while hunting, the blood was to be drained and covered with earth. All of this special treatment and respect for blood is explained in this chapter. "For the soul of the flesh (the soul which gives life to the flesh) is in the blood, and I have given it to you upon the altar, to make an atonement for your souls" (v. 11). First, note that blood was said to contain the soul of the animal; and secondly, as a consequence God had set apart the blood as the means of expiation on the altar (that is, sprinkled or poured on the altar. The animal's soul was offered on the altar as a substitute for the human soul.

Every bleeding sacrifice has an expiatory power. "The life of the flesh is in the blood." There it is. The innocent takes the sin and place of the guilty. Thus, sin is expiated and God and man are reconciled. God provided propitation for man so they (Holy God and sinful man) can talk face-to-face.

Pre-Session Assignment for Lesson 6

Regulations Concerning the People (18-20)

We now begin the part of the book that spells out God's expectations of His people and their lifestyle. He will do so by pointing out how the lifestyle He requires is different from those people around them. This will require a new way of thinking and believing. This is always true as we confront the accepted cultural and sociological norms for behavior. Cultural assumptions are not normally the result of an analytical process, they are simply embedded within us. God does not address what is culturally accepted when it is not in direct conflict with what is consistent with His character.

1. Chapter 18 is an outgrowth of the seventh commandment which is meant to call us to respect marriage and human sexuality. How did mankind become sexual beings?

2. Does God set parameters (boundaries) around sexuality?

3. Is all sex within the confines of marriage acceptable behavior? Is a marriage to a close relative (mother, father, brother, sister) acceptable (18:6)?

4. What do you think the Hebrew idiom (picturesque language), "you shall not uncover the nakedness of," means?

5. What sexuality other than kinship sex is condemned?
    v. 19 -
    v. 20 -
    v. 21 -
    v. 22 -
    v. 23 -

6. Chapter 19 predominately focuses on the fourth and fifth commandments and thus encompasses "loving God and loving neighbor." Comment on the emphasis on the two commandments:
    19:3a -

    19:3b -

7. Describe the welfare system God installs for Israel (19:9, 10).

8. List other ways to show love of neighbor as given in the chapter 19.

9. What does the chapter teach about spiritism and prostitution (vv. 26-31)?

10. Summarize the prohibitions and penalities of chapter 20.

Lesson 6 Regulations Concerning the People (18-20)
(Sexual and Social Holiness)

Now that they have the solution to the "sin problem" that separated them from a Holy God (chapters 1-17), God begins to speak to the people about how they should live. He does not begin with feasts and Sabbaths or even rules about making vows. The first thing He addresses is sex. We have seen that the issue of proper foods is placed in the sacrificial section of the book because it typified the thought-life of the believer. It spoke of how feeding on certain thoughts would render one unfit for God's presence. Now, God begins to address things that will destroy the person: first and primarily, the misuse and abuse of one's sexuality. Sexuality is a resource given by God to man to enable him to fulfill God's design for him. That is implicit in the statement of Genesis 1:28, "be fruitful and multiply and fill the earth." In order to insure this would naturally occur God designs the human body not only to desire such relationships but even more to enjoy the act of sexual intercourse. It was God Who made the intricate nerves, hormones, and neurochemicals necessary to the enjoyment of the sexual act. But He intended that man rule his passions as he was to rule the world around him. Sinful man perverted that which was designed for his own good by using it in ways inconsistent with God's design. When human sexuality is so misused it becomes deadly to the user and to his society.

The New Testament reinforces this idea and thus we know that these prohibitions given in the law are not spiritualized or set aside. They, like the Ten Commandments, are statements revealing the mind of the Lord on certain subjects. Please note the words of Paul in 1 Corinthians 6:15-20,

> *Do you not know that your bodies are members of Christ? Shall I then take away the members of Christ and make them members of a harlot? May it never be! Or do you not know that the one who joins himself to a harlot is one body with her? For He says, "The two will become one flesh." But the one who joins himself to the Lord is one spirit with Him.* ***Flee immorality. Every other sin that a man commits is outside the body, but the immoral man sins against his own body****. Or do you not know that your body is a temple of the Holy Spirit who is in you, whom you have from God, and that you are not your own? For you have been bought with a price: therefore glorify God in your body.* NAS

To sin against the body (God's temple) would be the equivalent of painting graffiti on the temple or vandalizing the temple. Israel was to go into a land whose culture was absolutely foreign and hostile to the culture God prescribed for them. These people worshipped deities that fought, killed, fornicated and practiced homosexuality, bribery, and committed robbery. These people were portraying gods who were much like themselves.

*The idols of the heathen are silver and gold, the work of men's
    hands.*
*They have mouths, but they speak not; eyes have they, but they
    see not;*
*They have ears, but they hear not; neither is there any breath in
    their mouths.*
*They that make them are like unto them: so is every one that
trusteth in them.* Psalms 135:15-18.

These prohibitions are not just a reaction to the new neighborhood, but they are about a worldview. Victor Hamilton quotes John Oswalt, "the rationale behind the ethic is not simply a reaction to a life style that happens not to be Hebrew . . . . Rather these activities are prohibited because they grow out of and lead to a world view that is radically opposed to that of the Bible . . . they represent one common outlook on sex and the world, that is, the denial of boundaries (1982 p. 302)."

There it is–boundaries or parameters. God is the only one who has the right to set the policies for the use of a thing. He has that right for He is the owner. He is holy and righteous. Therefore, all that He says or does is holy and right.

Holiness! That is the basic subject of this book. The word holy occurs in this book more than in any other. Strong's *Exhaustive Concordance* lists 90 uses of the word "holy" in Leviticus and 17 uses of the word "sanctification." The majority of these occur in chapters 19-27. The Hebrew root for the concept of holy, *q-d-sh*, occurs in one of its grammatical forms 150 times in Leviticus.

The word "holy" means "to set apart from _____ to God. It means that someone or something belongs to God. So holiness is primarily about ownership. It is about declaring that God is my Lord and Owner. As the owner He has the right to set boundaries or policies regarding how I will manage that which He has placed in my trust. To the extent that I do this within His parameters, I live in the context of holiness.

THE KEY = HOLINESS MEANS LIVING LIKE I BELONG
TO GOD!

Holiness then, means understanding that SEX is meant to be holy for the believer. Leviticus 18 leaves no doubt what holy sex is.

The terms and the language should be defined:
- Incest: sexual relations and/or marriage to any "close relative" ('*None of you shall approach any blood relative of his to uncover nakedness; I am the LORD*' v. 6 NAS). These prohibitions were new to Israel. Abraham was married to his half-sister and Moses' father was married to his aunt. There were multiple wives as well. However, in creation God had set a pattern for marriage—one man to one woman. The instructions now required that spouse (sexual partner) must be from outside the immediate group of relatives.
- Fornication and adultery: sexual relations with a partner other than one's spouse.
- Homosexuality: sexual relations with a person of the same sex.
- Bestiality: sexual relations with a non-human (i.e., animal, bird, etc.)
- Uncovering the nakedness of: a Hebrew idiom and euphemism meaning to have sexual relations.

Note the reason given for the prohibition in Leviticus 18:24-30.
'Do not defile yourselves by any of these things; for by all these the nations which I am casting out before you have become defiled. 'For the land has become defiled, therefore I have visited its punishment upon it, so the land has spewed out its inhabitants. 'But as for you, you are to keep My statutes and My judgments, and shall not do any of these abominations, neither the native, nor the alien who sojourns among you (for the men of the land who have been before you have done all these abominations, and the land has become defiled); so that the land may not spew you out, should you defile it, as it has spewed out the nation which has been before you. 'For whoever does any of these abominations, those persons who do so shall be cut off from among their people. 'Thus you are to keep My charge, that you do not practice any of the abominable customs which ave been practiced before you, so as not to defile yourselves with them; I am the LORD your God.' " NAS

God's idea of ecology is vastly different from that of man's. The nations have defiled the land through these abominations. That was why they were being forced out of the land. God informs Israel, "Don't you do these prohibited things or the land will vomit you out of it as well as it did them."

CHAPTER 19 Social Customs to Practice
In chapter 18 we learn what holiness is not and in this chapter we learn some positive sides of holiness. The phrase "I am the Lord" occurs 13 times as opposed to five in chapter 18. This repeated use underscores the concept that these laws are rooted in the holy nature of God Himself.

We see that holiness will be best demonstrated in one's relationships. It is addressed in relational terms. As they relate...

- To parents (v. 3) *"reverence father and mother and keep my Sabbaths"*
- To children (v. 29) *Do not profane your daughter by making her a harlot, so that the land may not fall to harlotry, and the land become full of lewdness.*
- To God
  'Do not turn to idols or make for yourselves molten gods; I am the LORD your God. 'Now when you offer a sacrifice of peace offerings to the LORD, you shall offer it so that you may be accepted. Leviticus 19:4-5 NAS

  'Do not turn to idols or make for yourselves molten gods; I am the LORD your God. 'Now when you offer a sacrifice of peace offerings to the LORD, you shall offer it so that you may be accepted. Leviticus 19:4-5 NAS

  'You shall not eat anything with the blood, nor practice divination or soothsaying. 'You shall not round off the side-growth of your heads, nor harm the edges of your beard. 'You shall not make any cuts in your body for the dead, nor make any tattoo marks on yourselves: I am the LORD. Leviticus 19:26-28 NAS

  'Do not turn to mediums or separatists; do not seek them out to be defiled by them. I am the LORD your God. 'You shall rise up before the grayheaded, and honor the aged, and you shall revere your God; I am the LORD. Leviticus 19:31-32 NAS

- To the poor and the stranger (God's welfare program) (vv. 9-10, 15, 33-34).

- To slave women (vv. 20-22).

- To one's neighbor or brother (vv. 11-18, 35-36).

- To the aged (v. 32).

- To animals (v. 19).

- To the land [soil] (vv. 19, 23-25).

The best known verse of this chapter is Leviticus 19:18 '*You shall not take vengeance, nor bear any grudge against the sons of your people, **but you shall love your neighbor as yourself; I am the LORD** (NAS)*. This verse is quoted nine times in the New Testament. This chapter says that it is not enough to love your neighbor but one must also love the stranger and sojourner as himself.

CHAPTER 20 Prohibitions and Penalties
Chapter 20 relates to the content of chapter 18 by revealing the penalties for forbidden behavior. Primarily, death is prescribed for most violations. This speaks to us that if people engage in these practices death and destruction will befall them. If they commit adultery, no one may stone them, but destruction will come.

There is also a stern warning about sacrificing children to Molech. This was a form of worship where the sacrifice of a child is to assure the "good life" for the person. Abortion and family neglect are ways of doing Molech worship today. Children are sacrificed because they are inconvenient; they are sacrificed for drugs or money. In some way they suffer to produce the "good life" for someone else.

It is clear that God wants His people to be different from all other people. His people are to live in such a way as to make it obvious that their ways did not come from the common culture. Christians should stand out in the crowd. They should not have a divorce rate equal to that of the world around them. They do not mistreat or physically abuse their spouses or children. They do not lie or steal.

Holiness, as it is presented here, is not a standard about dress or what one sees or hears. That was addressed in the chapters relating to forbidden foods. Here holiness is about how one relates to family and neighbors. Hebrews 12:14, "Follow peace with all men and holiness . . . ." They go together: peace with men and holiness.

Pre-Session Assignment for Lesson 7

Regulations for Priests and Other Regulations (21-22)

1. Compare the mourning requirements for priests (21:1-4) to those for the high priest (21:10-12).

2. Compare the requirements for a priest who wants to marry (21:7) to those for the high priest (21:13-15).

3. Should priests or those with greater responsibilities be held to a higher degree of accountability than those of less significant responsibilities? Give your reasons for your answer.

4. Should a Christian be held to a higher standard than an unbeliever?

5. Should one holding a ministry responsibility in God's house be held to a higher standard than those not holding such responsibility?

6. How does God feel about defective priests ministering and mediating on behalf of God and God's people (21:16-24)?

7. Is God concerned about people who have an unresolved defilement handling and eating of the holy gifts (22:2-9)?

8. Why do you think God gave such strict admonitions about the animal being offered (22:18-25)?

9. Rephrase and personalize the following verses:
   32 And you shall not profane My holy name, but I will be sanctified among the sons of Israel: I am the LORD who sanctifies you,
   33 who brought you out from the land of Egypt, to be your God: I am the LORD. " Leviticus 22:32-33 NAS

LESSON 7 Regulations Concerning the Priest (21-22)
(Leadership Holiness)

This second section seeks to focus our holiness of God's areas: our walk our worship, and our lesson investigated holy in one's walk. especially pointed at

Holiness in our
• Walk
• Work
• Worship
• Word

of Leviticus (18-27) attention on the people in four broad (lifestyle), our work, word. Our last what it meant to be God's interest was a most intimate and

powerful force in our lives—our sexuality. We saw that the abuse of sexuality (fornication, incest, homosexuality, and bestiality) led to the loss of life. It led the person to being "cut off" from among the people. This pattern is confirmed in the New Testament. Sexual sins are an assault on the body (temple of the Holy Spirit). Sexual immorality will prevent one from being a part of God's kingdom according to Gal 5:19-21.

> *Now the works of the flesh are manifest, which are these;* ***Adultery, fornication, uncleanness, lasciviousness,*** *Idolatry, witchcraft, hatred, variance, emulations, wrath, strife, seditions, heresies, Envyings, murders, drunkenness, revellings, and such like: of the which I tell you before, as I have also told you in time past,* ***that they which do such things shall not inherit the kingdom of God.*** KJV

Now we turn our attention to the work of God's people. Here it is couched in terms of the priesthood, but for our benefit we will look at it in terms of leadership. I use leadership here in the sense of the power, potential and practice of INFLUENCE. All of us will influence other people during our lifetime. Someone(s) will desire to follow your example, your lifestyle, or your words.

Often when asked how a person is to be holy an answer will contain the following type of responses: "If one will do _____ and not do _____ he/she will be holy." The problem with that type of response is that it makes being holy about doing and not about being. The Book says "be holy for I Am holy." Holiness is about being something and out of that being one works and relates. It is not about doing something to become something. I conclude therefore, that holiness is a character issue.

> Ask yourself, "Is what I do or don't do because I am holy or I am trying to become holy by what I do or don't do?"

Leaders understand that communication is largely about body language (21:1-4). Therefore family members are identified on whose behalf a priest is permitted to be defiled (He is to be careful in his relationships to avoid defilement). Those are:

- Father,
- Mother,
- Son,
- Daughter,
- Brother, or
- Virgin Sister.

The reason is that a priest must maintain higher standard of behavior than others because he is a leader. The high priest could not defile himself even in the event of the death of his father.

The priest and his parents must be very discretionary in choosing his wife (21:7, 13-15). His choice of a mate will greatly influence, either positively or negatively, his ability to mediate and lead others. He was not to be joined to a harlot (probably an idolatry problem), nor a divorcee (her baggage will be a detriment to his leadership ability). He was to marry a virgin (excludes even widows as a choice). The explanation is that he was not to profane (secularize) his offspring, because it is the Lord who has set him apart. Stubborn and headstrong choices will neutralize and negate one's holiness as a leader.

Another instruction was concerning the shewbread. God is giving you bread and this why you need to be holy (Godlike character) (21:8, 21-24). Bread represents the Word of God from heaven. Holy leaders are those who value the Word to extent they willing to limit their own rights.

Holy leaders understand that how they dress and how they wear their hair are statements about their concepts of leadership (21:5,10). One should not expect to be a holy leader when he demands to have his own way. God's interest, not the fashion industry, should determine how one treats his own body (hair, clothes, beard, or marks on the body).

Leaders must give attention to their heart attitude and spiritual aptitude to assure there are no marks or sin infections that would exclude them from ministering to and for the Lord (21:17-24).

The working priest and the holy gifts—offerings and consumption of them is the subject of chapter 22.

Leaders honor the things that they offer to God (22:2, 3). We must never let the things of God become so familiar that we act in ways that will disgrace the name of the Lord. Leaders cut themselves off from the people of God when they handle the holy with dirty hearts and spirits.

God's provision for us is not to be taken lightly (22:4-9). Attempting to consume the good things from the Lord while defiled with bitterness, gossip, malice, hurtful speech, and so forth could be deadly (v. 9). Let the Word and daily repentance bathe the defilement away. Leaders use wisdom to discern with whom they will share the manna given them by God (22:10-16).

Leaders teach others by example and by mentoring the kind of gifts that are acceptable to God (22:17-33). We always offer to God the first and the best. We offer things without defects. God expects our gifts to be free from cruelty and violence (vv. 27-28). The reason for these instructions is given in the statement, "I set you apart to Myself (sanctified you) by bringing you out of Egypt."

Pre-Session Assignment for Lesson 8

The Feasts, Anointing Oil, and Shewbread
(Holiness in Worship) 23-24

1. What is the first "holy day" God wants Israel to remember (23:3)?

2. What is the first "feast" God mentions in this chapter (23:5)?

3. Discuss the Feast of Unleavened Bread and its requirements (23: 6-8).

4. What was to be done on the Feast of Firstfruits (23:10-14)?

5. What is the Feast of Weeks and why is it called such (23:15-21)?

6. When does *Rosh Hashanah* [Rosh Ha-shannah] or Trumpets occur (23:23-25)?

7. Write down the things you know about the Day of Atonement (23:26-32).

8. What is the last of the seven feasts (23:33-43)?

9. What were God's instructions about the holy oil (24:2-4)?

10. What were God's instructions about bread for the table of shew bread (2:5-9)?

11. The 24th chapter closes with a most interesting narrative about a person who blasphemed. Please rewrite the story in your own words.

LESSON 8: Feasts, Anointing Oil, and Shewbread (23-24)
Holiness in Worship

It is important to note that the form of government that God wanted Israel to have reinforces the concept that God is in control. Israel was to be a *theocracy:* i.e., God was her king, her only one. In order to make sure that they never lost sight of this fact God prescribed several special conditions for them. They were not given a standing army, their army was a home guard that often had no one to lead it until God raised a person up to do so. They had no central government. The only functioning governmental office they had was the priest. They had a temple rather than a capitol building. They would need no politician legislating new laws, all their core laws were in place.

Now God prescribes certain special times of which three will require that they are always linked to this place on earth and to His holy place. It will also give them a sense that all things are working on His timetable and not on man's schedule. In fact, these feasts and appointed times are important to all God is doing or will do. Holiness means trusting God's timing. God's will is not only about WHAT He wants done, but also WHEN He wants it done and with WHOM He wants it done.

> *When they therefore were come together, they asked of him, saying, Lord, wilt thou at this time restore again the kingdom to Israel? And he said unto them, It is **not for you to know the times or the seasons**, which the Father hath put in his own power.* Acts 1:6-7 KJV

There are seven special days mentioned in this 23rd chapter; three are said to be said to be feast (*chag* [hag]) days while the majority are said to be appointed times (*mo'ed* [moe-ed]*)*. In essence these are times and seasons. The Sabbath (32:3) is the first special day that God will talk to them about, and it is not one of the seven special days in this chapter. The Sabbath is a visible way of identifying Israel's covenant with God. It is a "Sabbath of rest" and doing work on this day would result in death.

On the following page the student will find Figure 4 showing the feasts in relation to both the Jewish and Julian calendars. Following that you will find Figure 5 which will contain a brief summary of the feasts and special days.

Figure 4 Calendar of the Feasts

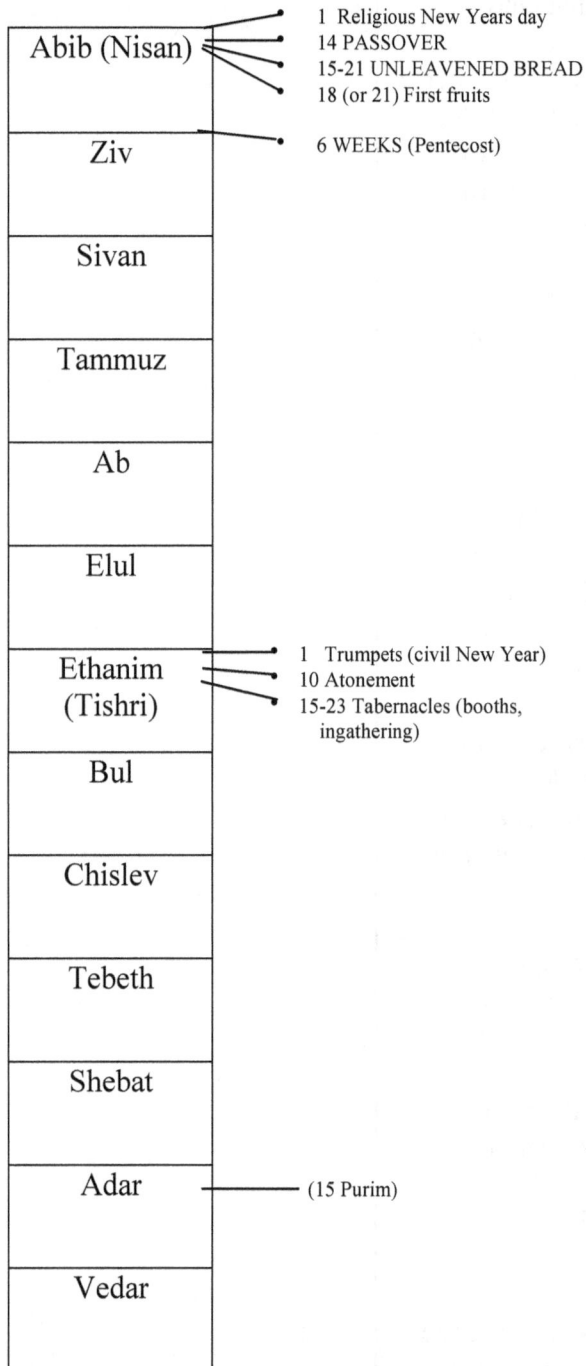

Hebrew Month	Feast	Gregorian Month
Abib (Nisan)	1 Religious New Years day 14 PASSOVER 15-21 UNLEAVENED BREAD 18 (or 21) First fruits	March
Ziv	6 WEEKS (Pentecost)	April
Sivan		May
Tammuz		June
Ab		July
Elul		August
Ethanim (Tishri)	1 Trumpets (civil New Year) 10 Atonement 15-23 Tabernacles (booths, ingathering)	September
Bul		October
Chislev		November
Tebeth		December
Shebat		January
Adar	(15 Purim)	February
Vedar		March

FEASTS AND SET TIMES IN THE OLD TESTAMENT[4]
Figure 5

NOTES

EVENT	PROCEDURE
SABBATH Ex 20:8-11; 31:12-17 Num. 28:9,10 Deut 5:12-15	1) Marked seventh day of each week, 2) Work stopped and people rest, 3) Daily sacrifices doubled.
NEW MOON Num. 28:11-15	1) Marked first day of each lunar month, 2) People rested, 3) Burnt, grain, drink, and sin offerings.
PASSOVER Lev. 23:5-8 Num. 9:1-14; 28:16 Deut. 16:1-7	1) Lamb slain at place of sacrifice, 2) Roasted and eaten by family, 3) Also unleavened bread and herbs, 4) All eaten.
UNLEAVENED BREAD Ex. 13:3-10; 23:15 Lev. 23:6-8 Num. 28:17-25	1) Unleavened bread eaten for 7 days and no new grain could be eaten until after offering 2) Daily offerings: burnt, grain, sin, 3) On 1st & 3rd days a solemn assembly was held.
FIRSTFRUITS Lev. 23:10-14	1) First barley sheaf waved, 2) Brunt, grain, drink, & possibly sin offerings are offered, 3) None to be eaten before this dedication.
WEEKS (Pentecost) Ex. 34:22; Lev. 23:15-21 Num. 28:26-31 Deut. 16:9-12	1) Wheat loaves waved before God, 2) Burnt, grain, drink, sin, and fellowship offerings are offered, 3) People rejoice, 4) Rest from work.
TRUMPETS Lev. 23:24, 25 Num. 29:1-6	1) Trumpets sound, 2) Work ceases, 3) Burnt, grain, and sin offerings.
ATONEMENT Lev. 16:3-34; 23:27-32 Num. 29:7-11	1) People fast and rest, 2) Burnt, grain, and sin offerings, 3) One goat slain, 2nd sent forth as scapegoat, 4) Blood within the inner curtain.
TABERNACLES (Booths, Ingathering) Lev. 23:34-43 Num. 29:12-38 Deut. 16:13-15	1) For 7 days people live in booths of tree boughs, 2) No work on the 1st or 8th day, 3) Daily burnt & grain offerings, 4) Bulls offered—one less per day, 5) Assembly on 8th day.

[4] Holdcroft 1996 p. 200

24:1-9 The oil and the bread
- The oil must be obtained by beating the olive. In this way a superior oil is obtained that burns without much smoke.

- Instructions for the 12 loaves of bread are given.
  o Each loaf had such large amount of materials in the recipe (2/10 ephah = 1/10 bushel) that they would have been quite large (one loaf would cover half of the table). The 12 loaves were probably arranged in two stacks on the table of 6 loaves each.
  o Whatever was not eaten in one week's time would be discarded and replaced by a fresh set.

24:10-23 Stoning the Blasphemer (took God's name in vain.)
- The son of an Israelite woman blasphemed God (his father was an Egyptian).

- In the name of *Yahweh* he cursed another man with whom he had a conflict. The narrative implies that in the heat of the fight this man showed verbal disrespect for God and a callous attitude toward his neighbor.

- He was put into custody in order that the leaders could seek the mind of the Lord as to what should be done.

- God's response was to review their system of justice: i.e., the system of penalties helped to establish the value of the victim for the Israelite society. In this case He demanded that they stone the blasphemer, thus elevating the value of respect for the holy.

Pre-Session Assignment for Lesson 9

Holiness and one's word (25-27)

Read these chapters and write your reflections on the value of God's word to you and the value of your words to Him.

LESSON 9 Jubilee and Vows (25-27)

Holiness in Work and Word

25:1-7 The Sabbath Year

Embedded in this new culture established in the covenant God makes with Israel at Mt. Sinai is the concept that God has provided everything they would need. They knew this was true because God rested after finishing His work. This is the importance of Sabbath. God's people needed visual aids reminding them that they had no need of anxiety for their provision because God had done it. Sabbath is to be practiced by observing a day in the week when no one did anything to provide for himself, and in this passage the Sabbath concept is expanded to include an entire year in which the people did nothing to make provisions. It is the sabbatical year. Its principles are as follows:

- They were to work the land for six years but in the seventh year the land and its produce (e.g., the vine) is to rest (25:4-5).
- This Sabbath was designed to provide the needs of all the people of God, especially the poor (25:6-7).
- God is determined to drive home the concept that His people are to trust that He has provided all they need and they can rest in his care. 1 Peter 5:7 *"casting all your care on Him for He careth for you."*

25:8-55 The Year of Jubilee

They were to count off seven sabbatical years (seven-sevens or 49 years). On the tenth day of the seventh month in the fiftieth year *the* blast of a "shophar" (trumpet) was heard as it announced that seven Sabbath years had passed and this was the year of grace. This day also marked the Day of Atonement (*Yom Kippur)* each year. This 50th year was the Year of Jubilee.

This mighty blast of the trumpet sets into motion a great release in freedom.

> *'You shall then sound a ram's horn abroad on the tenth day of the seventh month; on the day of atonement you shall sound a horn all through your land. 'You shall thus consecrate the fiftieth year and proclaim a release through the land to all its inhabitants. It shall be a jubilee for you, and each of you shall return to his own property, and each of you shall return to his family. Lev 25:9-10 NAS*

The following comment on Leviticus 25:8-55 is instructive

Verse 10. The words, "Ye shall proclaim liberty throughout all the land unto all the inhabitants thereof," are more closely defined by the two clauses commencing with hiy' (OT:1931) yowbeel (OT:3104) in vv. 10 and 11. "A trumpet-blast shall it be to you, that ye return every one to his own possession, and every one to his family:" a still further explanation is given in vv. 23-34 and 39-55. This was to be the fruit or effect of the blast, i.e., of the year commencing with the blast, and hence the year was called "the year of liberty," or free year, in Ezek 46:17. yowbeel (OT:3104), from yaabal (OT:2986) to flow with a rushing noise, does not mean jubilation or the time of jubilation (Ges., Kn., and others); but wherever it is not applied to the year of jubilee, it signifies only the loud blast of a trumpet (Ex 19:13; Josh 6:5). This meaning also applies here in vv. 10b, 11 and 12; whilst in vv. 15, 28, 30, 31, 33, Lev 27:18, and Num 36:4, it is used as an abbreviated expression for yowbeel (OT:3104) sh¦nat (OT:8141), the year of the trumpet-blast. (Keil & Delitzsch, Electronic Database 1996)

They were to know the identity of the One Who was really the owner. The heart of the lesson is Leviticus 25:23-24:

*'The land, moreover, shall not be sold permanently, **for the land is Mine**; for you are but aliens and sojourners with Me. 'Thus for every piece of your property, you are to provide for the redemption of the land.* NAS

Here is the principle, the land was the Lord's. He only loaned it to them to manage it for Him; to cultivate and guard it (as He instructed Adam and Eve). Behind it all, there are His lessons on redemption—the recovery of a lost thing.

Neither could a person own an Israelite. **A person cannot own what belongs to God**. He had purchased them with blood when He brought them out of Egypt. So, the rightful owner was returned to his land and the indentured servant was released from his obligations.

'And if a countryman of yours becomes so poor with regard to you that he sells himself to you, you shall not subject him to a slave's service. 'He shall be with you as a hired man, as if he were a sojourner; he shall serve with you until the year of jubilee. 'He shall then go out from you, he and his sons with him, and shall go back to his family, that he may return to the

property of his forefathers. 'For they are My servants whom I brought out from the land of Egypt; they are not to be sold in a slave sale. 'You shall not rule over him with severity, but are to revere your God. Lev 25:39-43 NAS

Birthright and inheritance are to be greatly valued. God's gifts are not to be thought of lightly. Remember that Esau did not value these things and it cost him dearly. God killed Onan, son of Judah, for despising inheritances. Hard times could come and one might need cash, so he would convert his inheritance into cash. His property would be placed at the disposal of another. But, property and Israelites could be redeemed.

There were three ways to redeem them. 1) A near kinsman (e.g., brother) could buy back the property and/or the person. 2) In case there was no kinsman or all kinsmen were too poor to make the ransom, the person could earn and save enough resources and could redeem it himself. 3) Jubilee would release the person and/or his property to freedom.

No one lost in this system. The purchaser bought the fair market value of what the land would produce until the next Jubilee. So, that upon reaching Jubilee he had reaped the full value of his purchase. In returning the property and persons to their rightful place and ownership both inheritance holder and purchaser are compensated. The terminal purpose of God for His people is presented in these pictures. They are redeemed and are destined to enjoy fully the inheritance that is theirs.

CHAPTER 26 BLESSINGS FOR OBEDIENCE
FAILURE FOR DISOBEDIENCE

Obedience to God's word is the path to the blessing (abundant living) of the Lord. Here in this chapter the Holy Spirit enumerates the good things Israel can expect as a result of obedience (26:1-13).

- He would send rains in their seasons.
  - The crops will be produced so abundantly that one crop will last till the next.
- There will be peace in the land.
  - They would sleep without fear.
  - The wild beast would not be uncontrolled.
  - Enemies would not successfully invade the land.
  - Israel would be successful in repelling adversaries.
  - Five of you will be stronger than 100 enemy soldiers and 100 of you will cause 10,000 to flee.

- God's favor would be toward them confirming the covenant.
  - ☞ Through abundant food supply,
  - ☞ Through God's dwelling among them,
  - ☞ Through God's claim of them as His people.

Leviticus 26:13 states that it was God's intention in removing them from slavery in Egypt to restore their dignity.

There is, as well, a listing of consequences of disobedience to the Word of God (26:14-33). [Note the recurrence of "seven-fold"]
- A sudden terror would be appointed over them.
  - ☞ Through wasting illness,
  - ☞ And due to their seed for planting being stolen.
- They would be struck down by enemies from whom they would flee.
- They would pay seven-fold for their sins.
- Their pride and arrogance would be broken.
  - ☞ Their pride in their power would be broken by the shutting up of the heavens and the closing up of the earth.
  - ☞ Their pride in their strength would be broken by the failure of their crops and vines.

Failure to respond to the Word of the Lord at this point would bring increased pressure with their plagues increasing seven-fold.
- Uncontrolled beasts of the field would take their children and their animals (herds).
- Their population would be reduced until they were unable to populate the land.

Further lack of response would meet a seven-fold increase of punishment in the following ways.
- Family stress would lead to cannibalism of children.
- Destruction of their places of worship would occur.
- Destruction of their cities would be accomplished.
- The people would be scattered among the nations.

A FINAL PUNISHMENT: God's purpose in removing them from the land was to allow the land to experience Sabbath (rest).

A FINAL WORD: **repentance causes the heart of God to be revealed and that heart is RESTORATION.**

CHAPTER 27 VOWS AND THEIR IMPORTANCE.

- Difficult or improper vows (e.g., sacrifice of children)
  - o Replace the vowed thing with money of equal value.
  - o Clean animals must be offered.
  - o Unclean animals must be redeemed with a substitute.
- Take care with promises and words.

CONCLUSION

One reason God gave the Law to Israel was to define the type of lifestyle He expected of the subjects of His kingdom. This lifestyle may be defined theologically as "holiness." It is instructive to us that when scripture lifts the veil of mystery that shrouds God's throne, the creatures most closely associated with that courtly scene are inspired by God's holiness. These cherubim do not mention God's love or His power; they appear to be overwhelmed by His holiness.

When these beings trumpet "Holy, Holy, Holy" they may mean that this One is different from all others in that He alone always acts consistently with Who He is. He declares, "I Am God, I change not."

Then the pursuit of holiness for believers would mean to seek to behave in ways consistent with the new identity God gives the person who believes in His Son, i.e., to put on the "new man" (Ephesians 4:20-24; Colossians 3:5-11). Thus, holiness seems to be an identity matter.

Identity, biblically speaking, is not derived from performance but rather from a pronouncement made by the Father about the person. This is the implication of the first temptation of Christ as recorded in Matthew. *"And the tempter came and said to Him, "If You are the Son of God, command that these stones become bread." But He answered and said, "It is written, 'Man shall not live on bread alone, but on every word that proceeds out of the mouth of God'"* (Matt 4:3-4 NAS). Note that it was the identity of Christ as the Son of God that was called into question. Satan suggested that Jesus could ascertain whether that identity was true if He would transform stones into bread. Jesus countered by arguing that if God had declared it so then it must be true.

This appears to be the crux of holiness. Each believer is whomever God has declared him to be. He must live according to that identity. He cannot be like all who do not believe. He has been set apart to God to be like Him.

Holiness is at once the foundation from which the Christian life begins and is the process of the Christian experience. As Leviticus demonstrates, no part of one's life is excluded from the call to holiness. "I Am holy, therefore, be holy yourself," God speaks through the book. He did not say "become," rather, BE.

How fitting the order of these books known as the "Pentateuch" is. Genesis shows God's grand plan for mankind and how man fouled it up. Exodus shows how God set about to redeem mankind from his failure and reestablish his inheritance. Leviticus shows that until God's plan is consumatated He intends that His people be a special people in the earth.

I pray that you can never again look at the book of Leviticus as a boring read and non-relevant to your life.

Reference List

Baxter, J. S. (1960, 1973). *Explore the book.* Grand Rapids: Zondervan.

DeWitt, R. L. (1988). *Teaching from the tabernacle.* Grand Rapids: Baker Book House.

Hamilton, V. (1982). *Handbook on the pentateuch.* Grand Rapids: Baker Book House.

Holdcroft, L. T. (1996). *The pentateuch.* Abbotsford BC, Canada: CeeTeC Publishing

.

Keil & Delitzsch *Commentary on the Old Testament: New Updated Edition*, Electronic Database. Copyright © 1996 by Hendrickson Publishers, Inc.

New American Standard Bible. The Lockman Foundation. 1960, 1962, 1963, 1968, 1971, 1972, 1973, 1975, 1977.

Strong, J. *Strong's exhaustive concordance.* P C Study Bible v3.2F for Windows. © 1988-2001. Biblesoft: Seattle, Washington.

The Online Bible Thayer's Greek Lexicon and Brown Driver & Briggs Hebrew Lexicon, Copyright (c)1993, Woodside Bible Fellowship, Ontario, Canada. Licensed from the Institute for Creation Research.